GREECE
AND
TURKEY

Cultures and Costumes Series:

GREECE AND TURKEY

PAULA HAMMOND

MASON CREST PUBLISHERS

www.masoncrest.com

Mason Crest Publishers Inc.
370 Reed Road
Broomall, PA 19008
(866) MCP-BOOK (toll free)
www.masoncrest.com

First printing 2002

1 2 3 4 5 6 7 8 9 10

Library of Congress Cataloging-in-Publication Data available

ISBN 1-59084-437-8

Printed and bound in Malaysia

Editorial and design by
Amber Books Ltd.
Bradley's Close
74–77 White Lion Street
London N1 9PF

Project Editor: Marie-Claire Muir
Designer: Hawes Design

Picture Credits:
All pictures courtesy of Amber Books Ltd.

ACKNOWLEDGMENT
For authenticating this book, the Publishers would like to thank
Robert L. Humphrey, Jr., Professor Emeritus of Anthropology,
George Washington University, Washington, D.C.

Contents

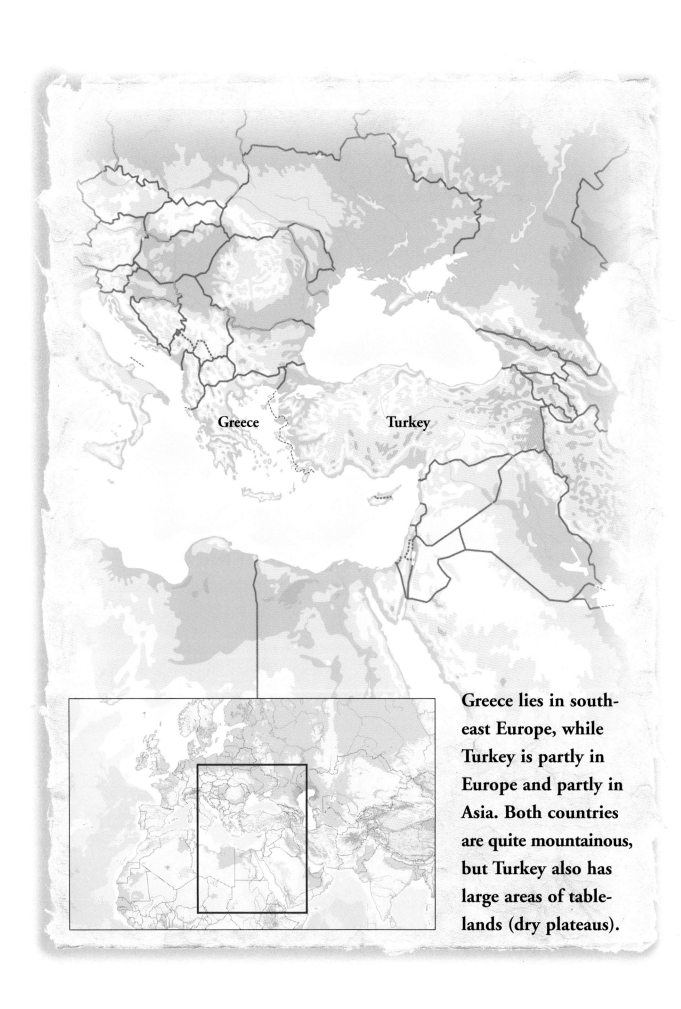

Greece **Turkey**

Greece lies in south-
east Europe, while
Turkey is partly in
Europe and partly in
Asia. Both countries
are quite mountainous,
but Turkey also has
large areas of table-
lands (dry plateaus).

Introduction

Nearly every species in the animal kingdom adapts to changes in the environment. To cope with cold weather, the cat adapts by growing a longer coat of fur, the bear hibernates, and birds migrate to a different climatic zone. Only humans use costume and culture—what they have learned through many generations—to adapt to the environment.

The first humans developed their culture by using spears to hunt the bear, knives and scrapers to skin it, and needles and sinew to turn the hide into a warm coat to insulate their hairless bodies. As time went on, the clothes humans wore became an indicator of cultural and individual differences. Some were clearly developed to be more comfortable in the environment, others were designed for decorative, economic, political, and religious reasons.

Ritual costumes can tell us about the deities, ancestors, and civil and military ranking in a society, while other clothing styles can identify local or national identity. Social class, gender, age, economic status, climate, profession, and political persuasion are also reflected in clothing. Anthropologists have even tied changes in the hemline length of women's dresses to periods of cultural stress or relative calm.

In 13 beautifully illustrated volumes, the *Cultures and Costumes: Symbols of their Period* series explores the remarkable variety of costumes found around the world and through different eras. Each book shows how different societies have clothed themselves, revealing a wealth of diverse and sometimes mystifying explanations. Costume can be used as a social indicator by scientists, artists, cinematographers, historians, and designers—and also provide students with a better understanding of their own and other cultures.

ROBERT L. HUMPHREY, JR., Professor Emeritus of Anthropology,
George Washington University, Washington, D.C.

The Ancient Greeks

An ancient legend tells the story of how the Greek god Zeus created the world. Sifting soil through a strainer, he spread rich earth over the land he had made.

Slowly, he created country after country, scattering the soil liberally to form lush farmland, rich forests, and rolling plains. After many days, the soil was used up, and all he had left were the stones and rocks in the strainer. These he used to make Greece.

Ancient Beginnings

Ancient Greece was a rugged, mountainous region that stretched from the southern edge of the Balkan Peninsula to the western arm of Asia Minor. The Greek mainland extends into the Mediterranean, and its hilly islands circle the Aegean, so that no part of Greece is more than 85 miles (137 km) from the sea. Greece was, and still is, a seafaring nation. Over a period of 600 years, Greek traders and conquerors used their **dominance** over the oceans to extend their influence into what is modern-day Turkey. By 479 B.C., ancient Greece was not

Ancient Greek ideals of beauty emphasized simplicity and elegance. This was particularly true of Greek costume, which utilized lengths of woolen cloth, draped around the body, to create simple but beautiful styles.

a single country, but a collection of many small ones. Each city-state, called a *polis*, was fiercely independent and patriotic. They often warred with each other but shared a common language, religion, and culture.

The Greeks considered the period from 477 to 431 B.C. to be their Golden Age—a time when art, architecture, and literature flourished. The richness of Greek culture was reflected in their clothing. The ancient Greeks made fine **textiles**, which they used to create some of the simplest and most elegant and imitated styles of clothing the world has ever seen.

Women's Work

Ancient people worked with natural materials to make clothes. In Greece, most households kept sheep and goats and used their wool to weave fabric. **Flax** was grown to make linen, and later, as prosperity and trade increased, silk was produced.

The weather is warm in Greece, with mild, wet winters and hot summers. Surprisingly, wool is an ideal material for this sort of climate. Wool that is coarsely woven can be heavy and warm. When woven into a fine material, it is soft and lightweight with a natural sheen. Such fine cloth can be easily draped over the body and, when worn in layers, drops naturally into the soft, flattering folds associated with ancient Greek clothing. The Romans admired this simple style of dress, as did the rest of the world. Versions of ancient Greek clothing can be seen today in traditional costumes of countries such as Ghana.

Cloth-making was a slow, painstaking process. Wool or flax was prepared for weaving by rolling it into long strands, either by rubbing the coarse fibers on the thigh or using a **spindle**. A special clay leg-protector, called an *epinetron*, was used in the rubbing method to avoid bruising and sores.

Women in ancient Greece had few rights. While poorer women and slaves worked in the fields, freeborn women could not even leave the family home without an escort. Yet weaving was so highly regarded that a widowed or divorced woman had the right to half of the cloth that she wove during the

Women and slaves were often barefoot, wearing sandals only when necessary. Some believe that this was to prevent their escape from the home.

marriage. Even the richest Greek women would be expected to have these skills. In a world where women, according to the historian Thucydides, should "not be spoken of," the greatest praise that a wife could receive was that she "worked well in wool."

Two Tribes

Ancient Greek culture was a vibrant mix of influences from two tribes: the Dorians and the Ionians. From these two different peoples came the main styles of Greek art and architecture: Doric and Ionic. These styles influenced all sections of ancient Greek life and can be seen in buildings, sculptures, and pottery, as well as in clothing.

The Dorians arrived in southern Greece, Crete, and Rhodes from the Greek mainland around 1200 B.C. As they spread across the region, they drove the Ionians out of their traditional homelands in the Peloponnesus into Attica and the western coast of Asia Minor.

The Dorians were a race of passionate warriors who valued discipline and honesty. The descendants of the Dorians ruled the powerful city-state of Sparta, whose people were famed for their **austere** lifestyle. The word *spartan* is still used today to describe something that is strict or without luxury.

It was the descendants of the Ionians who created the city-states and developed much of the philosophy, art, and literature for which ancient

Spartan Living

Athenians loved to laugh at their Spartan neighbors. One story tells of an Athenian noble who visited Sparta. On being fed a bowl of Spartan black broth, he declared: "Now I know why you do not fear death!"

Greece is famous. The center of Ionic Greece was Attica, which became the city-state of Athens. When we think of ancient Greece today, most of our images of the grand architecture, the Olympics, theater, and philosophy come from Athens. Generally, while Doric art can be seen as strong, Ionic art is graceful.

Simplicity and Elegance

The Dorians gave Greece its most enduring item of clothing, the **chiton**. Made from a long rectangle of finely woven wool, it was typically 18 inches (46 cm) longer than the height of the wearer and, in width, was double the distance from elbow to elbow. This length of material was folded over the body and pinned at the shoulders to make a short knee-length tunic. The *chiton* probably developed as a functional garment that could be made quickly and easily worn. The Ionians, with their fine **aesthetic** sense, developed and adapted it into an elegant, flowing garment that reflected their ideas about purity of style.

To protect the wearer from the cold and rain, a long woolen cloak called a *himation* was worn draped around the body. Men usually wore sandals or knee-length leather boots. Actors and acrobats preferred soft, tight-fitting footwear called *soccus*, which is where we get the modern word *sock* from.

A World of Color

Although we think of Greek clothing as white—as it appears on statues—the poet Homer talks of bright clothing colored with vegetable and animal dyes. Earthy yellows, vibrant reds, hennas, and rich browns and greens would have been common in clothing during the Greek Golden Age. Many *chitons* were decorated with a border that, when the material was draped around the body, gave the garment a patterned look. These borders could be elaborate, containing geometric shapes, flowers, birds, or even military scenes. These would either be woven into the cloth or painted directly onto the material by hand. The most commonly used **motif** was the Greek "key" pattern.

In ancient Greece, clothes were seen as a mark of social status, just as they

Occasionally, especially in Sparta, a short cloak of Doric origin, called a *chlamays*, was worn as the only item of clothing. A sun hat made of woven grass, called a *petasos*, and boots gave added protection from the elements.

The pattern that goes across the columns in this picture is an example of the Greek "key" style of decoration. This pattern was, and still is, widely used in Greek pottery and jewelry.

are in many parts of the world today. Although Greece was a **democracy**, only a small elite could take part in government. They enjoyed the best the ancient world had to offer, including the finest clothes. Some city-states even banned commoners from wearing certain types of clothes. In much of the ancient world, for example, royal or Tyrian purple could only be worn by the ruling elite. This was because the rich bluish-red dye was difficult and expensive to make. Over time, anything associated with this color came to be thought of as special, which is why, even today, ceremonial robes and carpets are red.

The vast majority of Greeks, however, were poor. Their clothes were adapted to the practicalities of working in the fields or on fishing boats. Working men wore plain, thigh-length *chitons*, with their hair cut short and covered by a small linen skullcap. This simple style of dress was so common that the Romans called farm workers *tunicati* after the short tunics they wore.

Ribbons and Gold

The great poet Sappho remembered with joy how her mother "was always exceedingly in fashion, wearing a purple ribbon looped in her hair." Clothes were important to women in the ancient world. For those who were wealthy enough, they offered a freedom of expression that was denied to them in other areas of life. Generally, women's clothing was more elaborate, brightly colored, and highly decorated than men's.

The female version of the simple Doric *chiton* was called the **pelpos**. This was a square, ankle-length piece of cloth pinned on both shoulders. Under Ionic influence, the *pelpos* became shorter, covering just the top third of the body, with a full-length *chiton* beneath. By the end of the fourth century B.C., this arrangement had become extremely elaborate. Layers of clothing were draped around the body and held in place by decorative pins or **brooches**. To accent the feminine shape, linen belts were tied at the waist and ribbons added under the breast. Extra brooches and material were added to form elbow-length sleeves, to change the shape of the neckline, or to give the wearer the appearance of a straighter, more elegant silhouette.

The careful use of brooches on a garment could produce a range of stylish variations on the simple *pelpos*. These decorated brooches were called *fabulae*, and up to 10 were needed to pin the material securely. *Fabulae* replaced the simpler, larger, Doric stick-pins. The reason for the change in style was

All Natural

Natural dyes are made from an amazing selection of ingredients. Tyrian purple is made from crushed **whelk** shells, while kermes, a rich red dye, is made from the crushed dried bodies of certain female insects.

probably that the *fabulae* were more secure and more attractive. However, the historian Herodotus gives a much grislier reason for the change in style. He tells a story of an army of Athenian soldiers who, having lost a battle, are executed by their enemies. One man manages to escape the slaughter and returns to tell the soldiers' wives what has happened. Distraught and angry at the death of their loved ones, the women pull the pins from their clothes and stab to death the unfortunate bringer of bad news. From that time on, Herodotus claims, the Doric pin was banned.

Greek women loved to dress their hair, tying it up with fillets and adding flowers, tiaras, or a diadem for decoration. To preserve their modesty, rich women would often wear a veil or hood over their hair in public.

Warrior Women

In contrast to the wealthy, perfumed women of Attica, women in Sparta were encouraged to see themselves as warriors, and they dressed accordingly. Spartan women enjoyed greater freedoms than women anywhere else in Greece and were encouraged to be active in business and public life as well as in the home. According to the philosopher Aristotle, women owned two-fifths of the land in Sparta. This freedom was reflected in their choice of clothing. Ancient sculptures show Spartan women wearing short, off-the-shoulder *chitons*, similar to those worn by the men.

> # Nips and Tucks
>
> In a radical form of ancient cosmetic surgery, Amazons were believed to cut off their right breast so that they could pull their bows more effectively.

In the epic tale of *The Iliad*, Homer tells of another group of warrior women from Asia Minor called Amazons. Although no one knows if Amazons really existed, images of them appear frequently on Greek pottery from the seventh century B.C. on. They are usually shown dressed in Persian-style armor, which looked a little like chain mail. When worn with a short tunic, it looked like the Amazons wore pants—but it was at least 2,500 years before women in Western Europe enjoyed that freedom.

Heroes of Old

Tales of heroes and battles of old were told throughout the Greek world. Stories of Troy, Odysseus, and Herakles (Hercules) were recited at social gatherings, and most young Greek men dreamed of the day when they would have the opportunity to prove their worth in battle. Such tales encouraged loyalty to the *polis* and courage in the face of hardship.

By the fourth century B.C., some form of military service was compulsory for all men in most city-states. In Athens, males between 18 and 60 were required to take an active part in the defense of the state.

Styles of armor varied throughout ancient Greece. A warrior's allegiance would be easy to spot by looking at how he dressed, the weapon he carried, and the motif on his shield.

In Sparta, all male children were taken away from their mothers to begin military training at the age of seven. From the age of 12, a Spartan boy would be given just one item of clothing per year to wear. All their underclothes were taken away, forcing them to endure the winter without any additional protection. This was meant to make Spartan men strong and disciplined.

In Sparta, military rank depended on ability. In Athens, it was determined by social standing, as all soldiers were expected to supply their own equipment. Wealthy citizens usually served in the cavalry, as only they could afford chariots and horses. The middle class provided most of the infantry and were called *hoplites* after the tall, round *hoplon* shields they carried. Slaves were expected to supply nothing but their physical strength at the oars of the Greek warships.

For the Glory of the Gods

The Greeks saw warfare as a ritual act and, in the early centuries, soldiers fought naked. Later, heavy bronze armor was introduced. A typical Greek soldier weighed about 150 pounds (68 kg) and his armor weighed half that. During the Battle of Marathon, an Athenian soldier would have worn either a bronze bell-**corselet** or a leather **cuirass**, which was just becoming fashionable. The bell-corselet was made of two sheets of bronze, connected at the shoulders and curving out at the hips. The cuirass was made up of strips of leather plated with bronze to create the effect of overlapping scales.

Both leather and bronze body armor were worn over a knee-length *chiton*. Added protection was provided by a Corinthian helmet, which covered the wearer's face, leaving slits for the eyes and mouth. The lower legs were protected down to the ankle by bronze armor called **greaves**. Only the *hoplite's* spear tip and his short sword were made from iron. Although most of southern Europe was using iron by 1000 B.C., the Greek poet Homer said that it was rarer than gold. Most of the iron used in Greek weaponry was imported from Greek cities in Asia Minor.

Horace on *Hoplons*

Hoplons were cumbersome, and soldiers often dropped them when running from the enemy. For Spartans, returning home without a shield was disgraceful. Typically, Athenians had a more relaxed attitude. As the poet Horace wrote:

> *Some lucky Thracian has my noble shield:*
> *I had to run; I dropped it in a wood.*
> *But I got clear away, thank God! So hang*
> *The shield! I'll get another, just as good.*

The Crown Games

The Olympic champion Diagoras watched with pride as his sons won their own Olympic crowns. To a standing ovation, the sons hoisted their proud father onto their shoulders and carried him around the Olympic arena. On his head, they placed the wreaths of olive leaves that they had just won.

For the ancient Greeks, there was no finer achievement than to win at the great Games at Olympia. Athletes represented the peak of human achievement, and Diagoras and his sons had just joined that rare group of athletes who could claim to be the best. The only achievement that would equal this would be for Diagoras to reach Mount Olympus, where the Greek gods were believed to live.

The Olympics took place every four years. In theory, any freeborn Greek man could enter the Games, but athletes had to prove that they had spent at least 10 months of the year training, so only the rich could really afford it.

Because athletic events were held in praise of the gods, athletes usually

The chariot race was one of the most popular events at the Olympic Games. The designs on this chariot show the tradition of athletes competing naked.

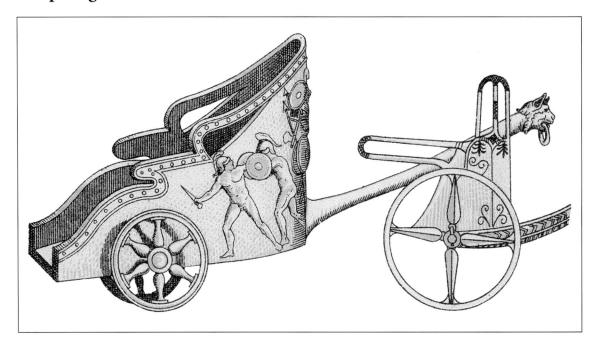

The poet Homer described how the goddess Athena took off the robe "she herself had made" and "armed herself for grievous war," with shield, plumed helmet, and spear, as shown in this traditional image.

competed naked, as Greeks viewed the male form as a thing of beauty and purity. Winners were crowned with wreaths: olive leaf at Olympia, laurel at Delphi, and parsley or celery leaf at Isthmus and Nemea. The symbolic nature of the wreaths ensured that athletes competed for the honor of winning rather than for financial rewards. Nevertheless, the prestige of winning was so great for the victor's home town that many competitors found themselves richly rewarded after the games. Food, olive oil, and clothing were given to winning athletes.

All the World's a Stage

Drama, like sporting events, had a strongly spiritual element in ancient Greece. Competitions in drama, dance, and music were held every year in many cities, and entries were usually serious or philosophical pieces.

Nowhere did costume represent culture more clearly than in Greek theater. Various masks showed the mood of the character and also allowed the same actor to play many roles. Clothes, too, were important symbols. Theatergoers accepted that an actor dressed in a certain way was portraying a particular hero or god. This was especially important when men played all the roles. Athena, as the goddess of wisdom and warfare, always wore a helmet and carried a shield and spear. Artemis, the huntress, wore a short *chiton* and carried a bow and arrows. Aphrodite would often appear nude, as befits the goddess of love.

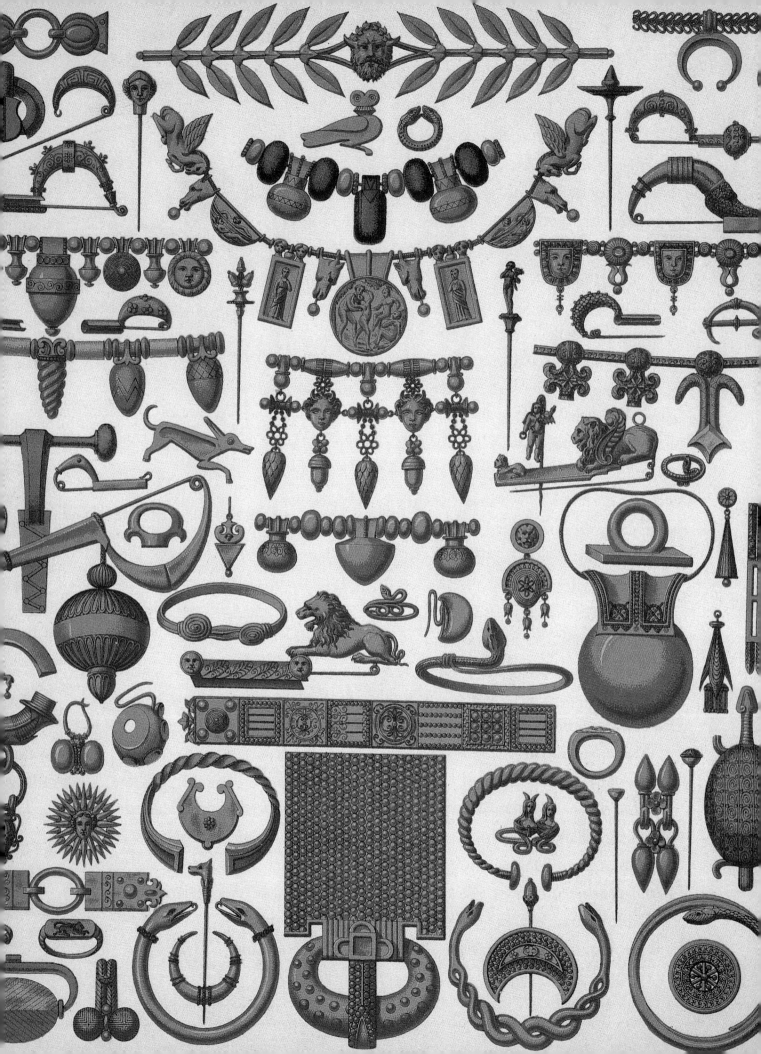

The Byzantine Empire

It is said that imitation is the sincerest form of flattery. The Romans saw ancient Greece as the height of civilization, and when, in 146 B.C., the armies of Emperor Antoninus Pius conquered the region, they were eager to learn from their new colony. Over the next two centuries, Rome adopted Greek ideas on art, literature, and clothing.

This process was called Hellenization, which means "to become like the Greeks." In fact, so impressed were the Romans with Greek culture that in A.D. 330, they established a "new Rome" in the Greek city of Byzantium, which they renamed Constantinople in honor of Emperor Constantine.

An Eastern Empire

Byzantium, on the site of modern-day Istanbul, was a natural fortress set on the Bosporus, a **strait** connecting the Black and Mediterranean seas. Looking east to Asia and west to Rome, it was an ideal defensive and administrative site from which to manage an expanding empire. With the fall of Rome, however,

This is a selection of Greek and early Byzantine jewelry made from gold, ivory, and enameled metals. Greek *fabulae* brooches (upper right), remained a practical and decorative way of fastening clothing for many centuries.

Constantinople and the territories in the East were lost to the empire forever. This newly founded city was suddenly at the center of a vibrant eastern empire whose cultures and traditions came from 11 countries and many thousands of years of history. This new empire was called Byzantium.

While Western Europe entered the Dark Ages, Byzantium thrived, adopting new ideas from its Eastern and Asian neighbors. This blending of East with West did not happen instantly. The ancient world moved slowly, and during the first few centuries after the fall of Rome, the people of Byzantium continued to call themselves Romans and to look to the Catholic Church for spiritual guidance. It was only in the sixth century A.D. that Greek finally replaced Latin as the official language of the empire and a Golden Age of Byzantine culture began.

Rich and Poor

Byzantium had two periods in which the empire flourished. The first of these was under Emperor Justinian, from A.D. 527 to 565. The second was during the 9th to the 13th centuries.

Justinian was a passionate and intelligent ruler who was determined to rebuild the Roman Empire. During the 38 years of his reign, he embarked on a series of conquests that saw Byzantium's influence grow from the southern tip of Spain to North Africa. Trade, art, and architecture thrived under his rule, and much of what we know about the Byzantine people comes from the art produced at this time.

We know little about ordinary people in the empire. History has only been interested in the poor during times of war and famine. Life for the poor in the Byzantine empire probably changed little over the centuries. In the fourth century A.D., farmers still wore the same linen *chiton*-style tunics that their Greek and Roman ancestors had worn 1,000 years earlier. The only additions were **breeches**, which were tied to the legs with leather thongs, and heavy leather shoes. Farmers may also have worn a Phrygian-style sun hat for

The Roman *toga* was based on the Greek *chiton*. This image shows how this blending of cultures resulted in new styles of dress.

protection from the weather. (A Phrygian hat is conical in shape; similar ones were worn by peasants during the French Revolution.)

For the wealthy, Justinian's rule brought spectacular luxury, and this was reflected in the costly fabrics worn. Early in the life of the new empire, the draped style of clothes, copied by the Romans from the Greeks, remained in vogue for some time. But slowly, as trade with Egypt, Persia, and Russia increased, fashions began to change.

New Fabrics, New Styles

Greek and Roman clothes were made from wool and linen, which could be easily wrapped around the body. Eastern fabrics, such as cotton and felt, worked better when tailored to the body rather than draped.

For men, a straight **chemise** with long, tight sleeves was worn as an undergarment. On top of this was a Roman-style tunic, which could be knee- or ankle-length. Under the chemise, men wore breeches, which had been

This charioteer has his arms and legs completely covered with a long woolen undergarment. This style of dress was in stark contrast to earlier Mediterranean fashions, where large areas of skin would be left exposed.

introduced by Roman soldiers from a style worn by barbarian horsemen. All men wore long, knitted woolen hose, which reached the thigh and were held in place by garters. Cloaks in the style of the *himation,* or Roman circular cape, were still in use and worn draped over one shoulder. *Togas* also remained fashionable for public officials until the end of Justinian's rule. Byzantine *togas* were made of rich **brocade** and were much stiffer and less easy to drape than the original Greek or Roman garment.

Women's clothes echoed the men's. On top of the long chemise was a tunic, closer-fitting and tied at the waist with a **girdle** in the Greek and Roman style. Cloaks called *pallas* were worn draped on the shoulders and sometimes over the head.

Luxury and Excess

More than the cut of the fabric, what really made Byzantine clothes different from those worn in the West was the sheer luxury of the materials used. Clothing was generally patterned all over, with ornamental borders added around hems, sleeves, and collars. This style of decoration, called *clavi*, was popular in Rome. Possibly because less skin was left bare to wear jewelry on, pearls, strips of beaten gold and silver, and gold thread were sewn into the heavy, richly embroidered fabrics. Silk, too, was used more freely during this time. This added an extra level of luxury, which that meant Byzantine clothing was widely admired throughout the world.

As the centuries moved on, clothes became richer and less Western. The Persian **caftan** was adapted into a long formal tunic, called a *dalmatica*, which was fitted at the back and left open down the front. Breeches and hose became true trousers. These figure-hugging items were worn by both sexes, with long boots replacing sandals.

By 1180, Constantinople was a cosmopolitan trading center. Over 60,000 foreigners lived in the city, speaking 72 languages and bringing in $20 million a year in custom duties. The jewelry, expensive perfumes, and fine fabrics that Byzantine citizens enjoyed were an obvious display of the empire's success.

Learning the Secret of Silk

For over 3,000 years, the Chinese had kept the secret of silk manufacture from the world. Until the Japanese acquired the knowledge in the third century A.D.,

Coifed Curls

By the 12th century, Byzantine men usually wore short, neatly trimmed beards, a symbol of maturity and manliness. In earlier centuries, however, they would have let their beards grow down to their waists. They would then have braided or curled them, achieving the desired effect by sleeping with the braids in or with curlers.

China had a **monopoly** on production, which made silk more valuable than gold. The ancient Greeks and Romans imported raw silk from Persian traders at an enormous cost, but had no idea how it was made. So rare was this beautiful material that, in the Byzantine empire, it was reserved for royalty. This was a situation that Emperor Justinian was determined to change.

Over the centuries, merchants and spies had tried again and again to steal the secret of Chinese silk. Anyone found attempting to take the secret of silk to the outside world was punished by death. Knowing this, Justinian initially abandoned any ideas of stealing the secret. He believed that if he bypassed the Persian merchants who controlled the trade routes to China, silk prices would fall. It soon became clear, however, that this would not be possible. Just as the emperor was giving up, two monks came to his court. They had been working as missionaries in China and had seen the silk-making process. They described to him how the silkworms made their cocoons on mulberry bushes, and how the threads of these cocoons were used to make silk. Justinian offered them a huge reward if they would steal some mulberry seeds and silkworm eggs.

Finally, in A.D. 550, the monks returned with the silkworms and Justinian was able to begin silk manufacture.

Although Justinian guarded the secret of silk as closely as the Chinese, the impact on the empire was immense. Money flowed in from the new trade in silk. Byzantium now produced some of the richest clothing that Europe had ever seen. Silks were interwoven with gold and silver thread. Colored fabrics were made even more

Popular Purple

So exclusive had purple become by the 10th century A.D. that gifts of royal purple silk were highly prized and often given to diplomats to smooth over relations with neighboring states. The empress mother of Constantine, Saint Helena of the True Cross, was hailed as "Joy of the world, Glory of the Purple."

The richness of these silk, gem-encrusted, and embroidered German garments are clearly the influence of Byzantium on European states, such as Germany, which was then part of the Frankish empire.

extravagant with the addition of silk panels or silk embroidery. Women started to wear silk caps, veils, and hair ribbons. Samite, a strong thick silk, was used for heavier tunics and cloaks. For centuries to come, Constantinople would be the Paris of the medieval world.

Life in the Imperial Court

As Emperor-elect Michael V walked toward the cathedral of Hagia Sophia, where he would accept the crown from the reigning monarch, the eager crowd surged forward, unfurling before him **bolts** of purple silk. This expensive fabric was reserved exclusively for the imperial family, and Michael knew that merchants were forbidden by law from even selling "to persons who are strangers…purple of the distinctive dye."

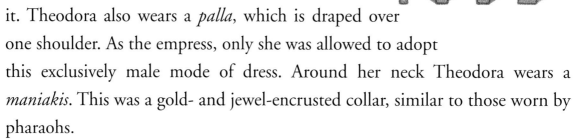

Emperor Nicephorus Botaneiates, who ruled between A.D. 1078 and 1081. On his head is a crown of gold, which was probably decorated with pearls and enameled panels showing images of Christ and the saints.

Purple was not the only exclusive element of imperial dress. The Church of San Vitale in Ravenna, Italy, shows a scene of Justinian and his Empress Theodora in full royal **regalia**. Following a popular style of the time, Justinian wears a long cloak, called a *paludamentum*, fastened over one shoulder. On the front of the cloak is a panel of richly embroidered and jewel-encrusted material. This was called a *tablion*, and only royals and members of their household were entitled to wear it. Theodora also wears a *palla*, which is draped over one shoulder. As the empress, only she was allowed to adopt this exclusively male mode of dress. Around her neck Theodora wears a *maniakis*. This was a gold- and jewel-encrusted collar, similar to those worn by pharaohs.

Although the colors of the mosaic in Ravenna have faded over the centuries, greens, blues, rich plum, and gold are still recognizable. The embroidery is exquisite, the jewelry extravagant. The imperial court was a dazzling place.

A World of Saints and Devils

From the beginning, the Byzantine empire was a Christian empire. It was Emperor Constantine who made Christianity the official religion of the Roman Empire, and after its fall, Christianity became the dominant religion of

A group of saints wearing symbolic rich red and purple clothing of the style common in the 10th century A.D.

the new empire in the East. In official images, the Byzantine Emperor is shown holding a military **standard** in one hand and a cross in the other as a symbol of his power over the Christian world.

Christianity permeated all aspects of Byzantine life. During Communion, called the Eucharist in the Orthodox Church, as the priest stepped forward to offer the sacred bread and wine to the congregation, he would say: "Approach with fear of God and with faith." For ordinary people, the spiritual world as represented in the Christian Gospels was real and inspired deep awe.

Belief in the power of evil called for protection. At the openings of clothes—around collars, cuffs, and hems—symbolic motifs were woven into borders to protect the wearer. For added defense against evil, amulets called *enkolpia* were worn around the neck. These were decorated with the images of saints and often held items believed to be religious **relics**.

Within such a deeply religious society, holy men and clerics had great

In the Orthodox Church, Patriarch was the name given to a bishop. The Bishop of Constantinople (the Ecumenical Patriarch) was the Church's spiritual leader. This ninth-century Patriarch wears a golden collar called a *superhumeral*.

power. Their style of dress made them a highly visible symbol of Jesus Christ and the Church.

A Symbol of Piety

Early Byzantine clergy followed the Roman style of dress. Typically, this was a type of *pallium*—a simple, Roman, draped tunic, similar to those worn by Greek philosophers. This was edged with a border of blue stripes, which told others that the wearer was a cleric. This color coding also applied to other professions: philosophers wore gray robes, and doctors wore blue. Early clergymen also shaved the crown of their heads in a style called a tonsure. Some Christian monks still wear their hair in this style today.

As the Church in the East became more isolated from the West, styles of clerical clothing changed. When we think of Orthodox priests today, we probably imagine an elderly bearded man dressed in long, flowing black robes with a tall black hat. However, religious paintings from the Byzantine period often show holy men and saints in red or purple robes. Rather than depict what they actually wore, the artist would indicate the high status of the figures by painting them wearing clothes associated with nobility. Holy men, then as now, wore somber, dark clothes as an outward expression of their **piety** and rejection of worldly things. Priests later adopted this simple style for similar reasons, although the black **cassock** and tall

The status of this ninth-century Patriarch as head of the Church is shown by the richness of the heavy gold- and silver-embroidered silks that he wears.

hat did not become standard clerical clothing until many centuries later.

The Clerical Elite

As members of the clerical elite, bishops and **patriarchs** dressed in the same type of rich fabrics and colors worn by the nobles. Styles varied greatly, with ceremonial robes worn during special Masses or at coronations. Typically, however, bishops wore a type of ankle-length tunic called a *stricharium*. A cloak was worn over this, as was an *omophorion*, a thin scarf draped over the shoulders and covered in crosses. This was often weighted at the bottom to make it hang straight. Patriarchs would sometimes wear a *superhumeral* rather than an *omophorion*. This highly decorated collar, rather like the imperial *maniakis*, showed the high status of the wearer.

Religious clothing is full of symbolism. The dominant colors worn by the clerical elite were red, gold, and purple. Red is a symbol of "ardent and active love." Many **vestments** also had ornamental borders on the hems showing Christian motifs, including fish, doves, and lambs, as well as geometric shapes, crosses, and flowers.

The wealth of these clothes can still be seen today. Tucked away in churches and monasteries in modern-day Islamic Turkey are mosaics and icons showing images of the people of Byzantium that remind us of the splendor of this once-powerful empire.

The Ottoman Empire: A Man's World

Western Europe had always been distrustful of the Byzantine empire. Since the Orthodox Church's split with the Catholic Church in 1054, the Pope had looked on Constantinople with suspicion.

In 1204, Western crusaders attacked Constantinople. The city was treated with such ferocity that modern historians call it "the Rape of Constantinople." Battered, the imperial court fled to Nicaea. It was 60 years before they returned to Constantinople. By this time, the once-great empire was crumbling.

A New Empire is Born

At the coronation of John V, a European visitor commented that most of the imperial garments were made, not of fine gold and gems, but of gilded leather

Harem (meaning "forbidden") was the name given to the women's quarters in the imperial palace. This image of life in a harem shows imperial women dressed in the type of embroidered waistcoats and silk trousers fashionable during the mid-1800s.

Ottoman Turks were Muslims. Like many religions, Islam requires its followers to dress modestly. Turbans, made from lengths of cloth wrapped around the head, were one of the most popular forms of headdress.

and polished glass. By the time of Emperor Constantine XI, the city was a shadow of its former glory. After centuries of war, even the city's richer inhabitants struggled to keep up appearances. Tourists described them as "sad and poor."

Finally, in 1453, Sultan Mehmed II, leader of the great Ottoman Empire, captured Constantinople and made it his capital. True to prophecy, Constantinople fell—as it had begun—with an emperor named Constantine on the throne. Constantine's last act was to throw off his imperial robes and, dressed as an ordinary soldier, seek death in the anonymous ranks of the city's defenders. This was not just an act of bravery. By removing his royal purple robes, Constantine was symbolically allying himself with the ordinary citizens.

Just as Constantine had once claimed Constantinople for Christianity, Mehmed II, the city's conqueror, now claimed it for Islam. With the addition of Byzantium's territories, Mehmed became the leader of an immense empire whose customs, culture, and clothing dominated Eastern Europe and Asia Minor until the beginning of the 20th century.

Bringing Order to Chaos

If you could go back 400 years and stand in the center of Constantinople, you would see an amazing blend of history and culture. Dominant on the skyline

These images, from the mid-1800s, show how the long flowing robes originally worn by the Ottoman nomads remained a feature of clothing for Turkish men within the Ottoman Empire.

would be the great Byzantine domed cathedral of Hagia Sophia (now a **mosque**). To left and right would stand the tall, elegant Anatolian **minarets** from where the **imams** would call faithful Muslims to prayer. Most glorious of all would be the newly built mosque of Süleyman I, built in the Persian and Arabic styles then favored by Islamic architects. Around the markets and trading centers, Greeks, Jews, Russians, Arabs, and Muslims would mingle freely as they went about their daily routines.

The Ottoman Court included many officials. Here, third from the left, is the chief eunuch; next to him, the aga, who was leader of the janissaries, and, far right, a vizier. The fur lining on their robes shows their high status.

It was this extraordinary blend of cultures and traditions that Mehmed II strived to arrange and classify. Within the Abode of Bliss, which was both his harem and his seat of power, the sultan's laws determined every aspect of life. This included specifying the exact dress that should be worn by leading families, court officials, and religious leaders. Mehmed II even specified the cut of the tunic, style of the turban, and length of the beard.

Practical and Modest

The Ottomans were originally **nomads**. The clothes they wore had to be easy to move around in and protect the wearer from extremes of the weather. Ottoman dress also had to be modest, as specified in the Muslim holy book, the Koran. This meant keeping the body and hair covered.

Clothes designed to be long yet comfortable in the hot, dry Turkish summers needed to be made from lightweight materials. Muslin, cotton, and silk are ideal for such clothes and were commonly used in Ottoman clothing.

Muslin was a fabric that was fairly unknown in the West during this time. Made from corded cotton, it was finely woven and light enough to be worn in layers. Poor families, who kept sheep and goats, wove their own fabrics in the home and used them to make simple garments, as had been done for centuries.

In the Byzantine world, status was easy to determine: richer people wore richer clothing. In the Ottoman Empire, despite differences in the materials used, the basic costume worn by Ottoman Turks made little distinction between the social ranks. Most Turks wore baggy pants, called **salvars**, that narrowed at the ankles. On the upper body, they wore a long tunic-style shirt with a heavier, embroidered *caftan* on top. The *caftan* was an ankle-length coat, open at the front and worn either loose or belted at the waist. By attempting to change and control what his citizens wore, Mehmed II made a greater impact on his people than any of his predecessors ever had.

Color Coding

Within Mehmed's dress codes, color was especially important. As the highest officials in the empire, **viziers** were the most extravagantly dressed. As specified by law, a vizier's *caftan* was green and his turban was white. For ceremonial occasions, heavier, primarily white robes were worn. These would be edged and lined with fur. As only the upper classes were allowed to wear fur, viziers often wore these robes year-round to show their high status. Mullahs, who were religious scholars, teachers, and leaders, wore robes of light blue. The religious elite, called the *ulema*, were allowed to wear purple. Chamberlains wore scarlet.

This color coding applied to footwear, too. Members of the vizier's staff, who worked just outside the court building, were expected to wear yellow footwear. Staff working inside the court wore red. To add a further dimension, Greeks had to wear black slippers, Jews blue, and Armenians violet.

Color coding even extended to members of the sultan's own family. During the circumcision ceremony of Süleyman I's three sons, Mustafa, Muhammad, and Selim were paraded before the crowd. Walking slowly and solemnly, they

The *fez* was introduced in the 19th century and took its name from the Moroccan town where it was first manufactured.

made their entrances one by one. The first was dressed in crimson, the second in red, and the third in gold. Each son could be immediately identified by the crowd according to the color he was wearing.

As the Ottoman Empire became richer, clothing **edicts** were increasingly used to reinforce social and racial divisions and to prevent ostentatious displays of wealth among the middle classes.

Turk-mania

In the farthest reaches of the Ottoman Empire, traditional Greek, Albanian, and Arabic costumes continued to be worn by the non-Muslim population, with adaptations made in line with the edicts of each successive sultan. In general, Ottoman Turks kept themselves separate from their non-Muslim citizens. Each foreign group was governed by its own leaders and lived within its own community, called a *millet*. Even with laws governing what could and could not be worn, a Christian or Jewish man would have been immediately recognizable in the crowd simply by the way he dressed.

To Westerners, fascinated by the richness and strangeness of Ottoman costume, Constantinople quickly became a byword for everything exotic. When, in 1720, a trade delegation from the Ottoman Empire visited Paris, "Turk-mania" swept Europe. Suddenly, everything that looked Eastern and exotic became fashionable. Constantinople became the place to visit. A famous painting of Lord Byron shows him in Albanian costume, with a gold and red brocade tunic and matching turban.

As a guidebook of the 1800s noted: "Constantinople is not one nation but many," and the richness of the style of dress made the exotic East seem even more so.

Turbans, *Fezzes*, and Hats

When we think of Eastern headwear, we probably think of turbans. Yet, within the Ottoman Empire, men's headwear could be tall, thin, brimless, squat, curved, plain, or highly decorated. Images from the period show a great variety of hats, some of them quite bizarre. In 1821, Reverend Walsh commented that, "Every covering for the head among the Turks seems remarkably ill-adapted to convenience." Even the turban, he commented, "in its best state…resembles wool sacks…balanced on the head like milk pails."

Nomadic tribesmen originally developed turbans to protect them from heat and dust, and they are still worn for this reason in parts of Africa and Asia today. *Turban* comes from the Persian word *dulband*, which is a scarf or length of material wrapped around the head. Within the Ottoman Empire, turbans were the dominant headwear for many centuries and, as with other items of clothing, rules determining the color, shape, and size of a turban helped signify the wearer's social status. While viziers could wear one heron feather in their turban, only the sultan could wear three. Green turbans indicated that the wearer was a *hajji* (someone who had been on a pilgrimage to Mecca). When Mahmud II (1808–1839) instituted his own clothing rules, only the clergy was allowed to keep the traditional flowing robes and turbans. Today, turbans are still worn as part of religious clothing, especially by leaders of the Muslim faith and followers of the Sikh religion.

Another common form of headwear within the empire was the *kalpak*. Many ancient paintings show lines of orderly court officials in long robes and tall, almost conical, hats. These *kalpaks* were made of lambskin and originated on the Russian steppes. Versions of these hats were worn all over the Ottoman Empire and came in many colors and fabrics.

Similar in shape, but shorter and stubbier than the *kalpak*, is the **fez**. The *fez* is a brimless red felt hat topped with a tassel of silk or wool. *Fezzes* used to be dyed red using the juice of berries found only in Morocco. Eventually, the *fez* replaced the turban as the everyday headwear for men in the empire.

Until the 20th century, Ottoman military uniform was dominated by styles adapted from those worn by hillmen and nomads. They were made from durable woolen cloth.

Slave Soldiers

Ottoman armies were huge, and their soldiers varied widely in appearance, depending on the region that they came from. It is the **janissaries**, however, who best represent what a typical Ottoman soldier looked like, as they formed most of the infantry by the reign of Süleyman I (1520–1566).

Janissaries were originally slaves who had been captured in battle or given in tribute by defeated nations. Most janissaries were not Muslims, but were forcibly converted once they joined the army. Janissaries were the empire's professional soldiers and had a reputation as excellent warriors. It was the janissaries who stormed the walls of Constantinople and made the defeat of the Byzantine empire possible.

In battle, janissaries were equipped with weapons that were basic, but good—originally bows, but in later centuries, muskets. Their robes were also of good quality, made from heavy wool and extremely colorful.

On the battlefield, the janissaries made up a highly visible core, with their yellow and red ankle-length coats, patterned sashes, and cloths of white wool or linen folded on their heads. Their leaders were distinguished by even more extravagant costumes, particularly their helmets, which were "so tall and top-heavy that they are…obliged to keep them on with their hands." Janissaries were a living example of the splendor of the Ottoman Empire.

Whirling Dervishes

The janissaries had strong links with a mystical cult called the dervish. Dervishes were wild men who followed their own heretical form of Islam. They wore knucklebones around their necks and carried wooden swords as well as drums that they banged while they prayed. They often worked themselves into a frenzy by dancing in circles—hence, they came to be known as "whirling dervishes."

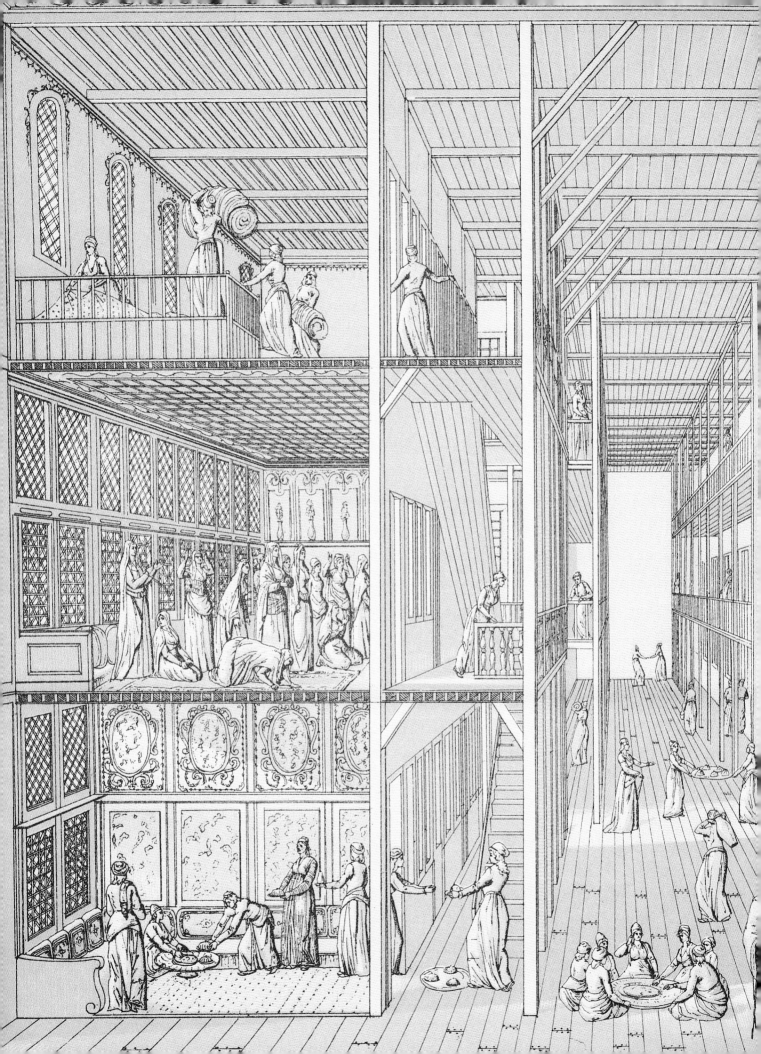

The Ottoman Empire: A Woman's World

As had been the case in Greece and Rome, life for women in the Ottoman Empire varied greatly with social status. Generally, non-Muslims and the poorer sections of society had fewer restrictions on the way they lived their lives.

Women from the ruling Ottoman families had their lives strictly regulated by custom. They lived a secluded life, mostly confined to the family home. They were required to be covered from head to foot when in public, and even at home lived in a separate part of the house called a *haremlik*.

A Private World

Many Westerners were outraged at what they saw as the "imprisonment" of Ottoman Muslim women. The American author William Elroy Curtis

This image, based on a drawing by the architect Ignaz Mellin, shows life inside the harem. Despite Western tales of harems full of scantily dressed women, in reality, the women wore practical, all-covering clothing, suitable for both work and prayer.

misinterpreted the cultural reasons for keeping women covered, believing "the idea of wearing the veil is to make women as hideous as possible...." In reality, the veil provided women with respect and a degree of freedom not enjoyed by their Western counterparts. The English writer Lady Mary Montagu, one of the first Western women to visit Constantinople, quickly came to appreciate the advantages of being veiled, declaring in 1717: "'Tis very easy to see that they have more Liberty than we have...no man dares either touch or follow a woman in the street."

Muslim women enjoyed great status within the home as mothers and daughters. Unlike other women in Europe at the time, they could also own property, manage and inherit money, and even divorce. Despite the rules on clothing laid down by successive sultans and the Koran, clothing, too, was far less restrictive.

When in public, Turkish women wore a **_ferace_**, which was a long, flowing, ankle-length robe. The _ferace_ was usually black and was designed to keep as much of the wearer hidden as possible. Muslin was used in layers to form a veil. One covered the face, except for the eyes; the other hung down the back to hide the hair.

This was the public image of Muslim women in the Ottoman Empire. However, beneath the _ferace_ could be a princess, a merchant's wife, horsewoman, or midwife, resplendent in fine embroidered cottons or bright silks and wearing the latest hairstyle. While European women squeezed their bodies into corsets that were sometimes so tight that the wearer fainted, typical Ottoman clothing was comfortable as well as elegant.

Beneath the Veil

In style, basic Ottoman women's clothing was similar to that worn by Ottoman men. Typically, this meant wide _salvar_-style pants worn under a long tunic called a chemise. On top of this would be an _entari_, which looked like a long waistcoat that was tailored at the back and left open at the front. The _ferace_ and

When in public, Muslim women wore long flowing robes that hid the shape of the body. Veils covered the head and face, leaving only the eyes visible to the observer.

veil would only be worn outside. Except for their immediate family and husbands, Muslim women spent most of their time with female relatives—and in the company of women, they could dress to please themselves.

Beneath the *ferace* were *salvars* made from fine embroidered silks. Chemises were beautifully patterned and fastened at the neck with jeweled brooches. Diamond and pearl buttons were added to richly lined silk *entari*. In the winter, heavy caftans were also worn. These were lined with furs imported from Russia. To this was added wide belts of linen or silk, which, if the wearer was especially wealthy, would have buckles.

Footwear, called *babusch*, was made from soft leather in a wide range of colors. An indoor version was often embroidered with silk and gems. Jewels, gold, and silver were used wherever possible. Ottoman taste in ornamentation favored the big and showy. Mirrors and goblets were often so encrusted with gems that it was hard to tell what the original purpose of the object was. Jewelry tended to follow this fashion, as well, with large displays of pearls and diamonds, particularly in headwear. Lady Montagu again gives us a description of just one of the many varieties of hats in fashion: "a cap fixed on one side of the head, hanging a little way down with a golden tassel and bound with a circle of diamonds."

For poorer women, an edict of 1564 specified that simple tunics, a veil, and a long skirt should be worn. These skirts were called *gömlets* and were made of wool or a cheap mix of cotton and silk, called *beledis*. This style of clothing was common among poorer Turkish and non-Turkish women throughout the empire (it is still the traditional rural dress in many parts of modern Turkey, Russia, and Greece). Occasionally, non-Muslim women, in keeping with local customs, wore a veil or head scarf. In Constantinople, non-Turkish women usually had their heads covered, but faces showing. In Athens, unmarried women were veiled, but married women were not.

When in private, wealthy Muslim women enjoyed wearing all the latest fashions, which, after 1860, included Western-style gowns made from imported rather than homemade silks.

Within these broad styles, all women adapted clothing to suit the local climate and materials available. Clothing restrictions could not be ignored, but they could be stretched. Greek women, for example, might wear dark blue or green footwear rather than the specified black. *Feraces* might be edged with embroidery, lined with silk, or dyed red or lilac. This resulted in a fantastic array of costumes that delighted tourists.

Life in the Imperial Palace

When Mehmed II built his palace on Seraglio Point, he gave orders that it should "outshine all and be more marvelous than the preceding palaces in looks, size, cost, and gracefulness." Located close to the site of the old Byzantine **acropolis**, the palace was a place of beauty and grandeur. Within, the sultan and his family enjoyed a life of luxury in which over 600 potters, jewelers, and weavers worked continually to create and maintain this monumental symbol of Ottoman power.

Ceremony dominated life within the palace. In the women's quarters, the queen mother, called the *valide sultan*, carefully supervised every aspect of daily routine. She was appointed by the **kethüda**, whose symbol of office was a silver mace. In charge of the laundry was the *çamasir*, who ensured that all imperial clothing was washed correctly. The food taster, typically dressed in red *salvars* and a long tunic, ensured that the food was served well and untainted.

Within the secret world of the sultan's women, dozens of attendants, slaves, and servants moved silently and efficiently through their daily tasks. Slaves in the Ottoman Empire were generally treated well and could expect rewards for

New Outfit

Lady Mary Montagu, who visited Constantinople in 1717, was so delighted with Turkish fashions that she immediately bought herself a complete costume. This she wore with delight, abandoning the restricting corset and hooped skirt that her Turkish hosts believed she had been locked up in by her husband.

As Islam required women to be modestly dressed, Ottoman Turkish dancers used this to their advantage, wearing layers of brightly colored clothing that emphasized the graceful movements of the dancer.

faithful service. Many of the women slaves had been given as gifts by visiting dignitaries and came from all over the world. These women were expected to be beautiful as well as skillful. In return for their service, they were paid a salary and given other gifts. These included at least three dresses per year, including one of silk, and material for shirts and handkerchiefs. After nine years, these women were free to collect their accumulated wages and return home.

Music and dance were encouraged in the royal palace, and girls were taught these skills from an early age. The *köçek oyunu* and *tavsan oyunu* were complex dances requiring great skill (occasionally, they were performed by men dressed as women). The first of these dances required the performer to wear a voluminous skirt, called a *köçek*. In the other, black *salvars* were worn. In the privacy of the women's quarters, dancers had the time to perfect the skills required to move gracefully in such flowing robes.

Royal Women

Royal men were groomed from an early age to be leaders. They were fiercely competitive and often had their rivals in the line to succession—and occasionally their own fathers—murdered. Sultans' daughters, on the other hand, could never become rulers in their own right and so enjoyed a relationship with their fathers that was untainted with suspicion. They were

George De La Chapelle, visiting Constantinople in the 17th century, wrote about the women of the imperial palace: "These women can sing, dance, laugh, entertain, and invent a thousand amusements."

spoiled and indulged, enjoying days spent in the steam baths, playing tric trac (a form of backgammon), or shopping.

When a royal princess eventually married, she expected to continue to live in luxury. The bride would move into the groom's house immediately after the wedding. With her, she would take attendants, slaves, and a large and expensive wardrobe. A princess did not expect to wear the same dress twice, and maintaining this lifestyle demanded a rich and influential husband. Whatever the status of her husband, a sultan's daughter maintained considerable power in her new home. The symbol of the princess' power was the *hançer*, a small jeweled knife worn in the belt. From this, princesses received the title *haním sultan*, meaning "lady sultan." Even their husbands had to address them by this title.

Ottoman women may have had to hide their faces, but they still enjoyed many freedoms denied to Western women. As the centuries progressed and these freedoms increased, their power to influence social change also grew, and women increasingly saw opportunities to exert their influence outside the home.

The 19th Century and the Influence of the West

The Ottoman Empire had an expansionist policy. It warred constantly with its neighbors and had little time for diplomacy or compromise. By the 19th century, the empire stood alone as the major Islamic power in an increasingly Westernized world.

Its power, however, was crumbling. Wars, failed harvests, and increasing demands for foreign rather than home-produced goods were crippling the region. Within the empire, revolution was rife as Jewish, Armenian, and Greek rebels struggled for independence.

These two factors—the growth of nationalist feelings among the countries that made up the empire, and the growing impact of Western culture—were the main influences on Ottoman costume and culture in the 19th century.

These figures wear a selection of Ottoman Turkish costumes from the 19th century—an era that saw a change in traditional Ottoman dress. The *fez*, for example (upper right), eventually replaced the more traditional turban (lower left).

These men wear variations on the traditional *foustanella*-style skirt. The *foustanella* was originally made from panels of linen that were coated in thick layers of animal fat to keep out the rain.

The Fight for Liberty

During the 19th century, the culture of ancient Greece was still greatly admired in Europe. In 1827, Britain, Russia, and France agreed to join the Greeks in their struggle for independence from the Ottoman Empire. After much bloodshed, diplomacy, and compromise, this was finally achieved in 1829 when a Bavarian prince, Otto, was established as Greece's first independent ruler since the Roman conquest in A.D. 149. This still left over three million Greeks living in Ottoman-controlled territory and another 200,000 in the

British-administered Ionian islands. In their continuing struggle for freedom, costume became the focus for national identity and pride. This was particularly encouraged by Greece's first queen, Amalia.

Within the Ottoman Empire, Greeks wore a variety of clothing—from Turkish-style garments, to clothes that had their origin in ancient Greece. Amalia wanted to reflect this rich history, and eventually developed the costume that is still worn in parts of Greece as a national dress to this day. What is called "the Amalia costume" consisted of an ankle-length skirt—which could be a variety of colors, particularly pastels—worn with a plain white shirt and a jacket that was heavily embroidered with gold thread. A loose, tasseled red cap, called a *toque*, was worn on the side of the head by unmarried women. Originally just worn by women in Greece, the Amalia costume eventually became the costume of Greek women within Ottoman territories, too.

Costume for Greek men was also influenced by the fight for independence. Traditional costumes from the Peloponnesus and Attica included the *foustanella*. This was a white pleated skirt made from stiff linen. With this was worn a silk turban or *fez*, a short, embroidered waistcoat called a *ghileki*, and a broad sash tied around the waist. The sash varied in color, but generally black was worn by older men and red by younger. Shoes or slippers had a pom-pom, called a *tsatouhia*, attached to the toe. This costume became the official dress at

This man from the 1860s wears a *stambouline* and *fez* with traditional *salvars*. Men of this time also wore knee-length brown or black pants called *zivka*.

Women wore *fezzes* either with a veil attached or, as shown here, decorated around the rim with a string of coins that hangs over the forehead.

King Otto's court and gradually was worn by all Greek men as a symbol of their support for the revolution. The costume is still worn today by some Greek regiments and on weddings and special occasions.

With the help of King Otto and Queen Amalia, interest in Greek costume was revived and the new Greek nation developed a style of dress uniquely its own, which can still be seen today.

While Western fashions became the norm in cities by the middle of the 20th century, in rural areas, clothing is still identifiably Greek, and remains an important link with the nation's long and rich history.

The Fight for Survival

While the newly independent Greek nation fought to establish itself, the Ottoman Empire was struggling simply to survive. Although East and West had never completely trusted or understood each other, by the 19th century, the Ottoman Empire was trading in more than just goods with its European neighbors. It was also involved in a great cultural exchange that saw art, architecture, ideas, and clothing cross national borders. It was these new ideas that inspired the great reformer Mahmud II, who was determined to modernize the empire.

Mahmud began by abandoning all the old dress codes and replacing them with new ones. Out went the turban and caftan. In its place, he required all Muslim men to wear trousers and a *stambouline*. This was a frock coat that hung just above the knee and was named after the Turkish word for the Byzantium part of Constantinople: Stambul. Worn under this was a high-necked white shirt. A bright sash wrapped around the waist was used to hold purses or weapons.

The turban was replaced by the *fez*—a man's hat, but one that middle-class women also began to wear with style. Mahmud had originally considered a three-cornered hat, but rejected it on being told that the three sides were meant to represent Christianity's Holy Trinity. The *fez* was the ideal solution to the problem of a more Western style of headwear. It was tight-fitting and did not have a brim, so it would not be knocked off during prayer.

Although Mahmud's reforms were eventually pushed through, they were initially strongly resisted. The *fez*, particularly, took some time to establish itself. Even European visitors regretted the loss of such a grand item of national dress as the turban. One visitor, writing in 1834, commented: "The costly turban, that bound the brow like a **diadem**, and relieved by the richness of its tints the dark hue of the other garments, has now almost entirely gone from the streets."

Like the empire itself, these new clothes were not quite Western and not quite Eastern. They were a symbol of

A selection of clothing worn by Ottoman women in the mid-1800s. With new clothing edicts, many traditional aspects of Muslim costume were abandoned. For some women, the *fez* became an acceptable, and fashionable, alternative to the veil.

Mahmud's desire to bring change to an empire that he felt desperately needed it. Nowhere can Mahmud's vision be seen more clearly than in his new army, which he called the "Triumphant Soldiers of Allah." Borrowing what he saw as the best elements of Western dress, military strategy, and training, he created a new Ottoman army "on the European model, with Russian jackets, French regulations, Belgian weapons, Turkish caps, Hungarian saddles, English swords, and instructors from all nations."

With his clothing reforms came great changes in Ottoman customs and lifestyles. He abolished the janissaries and **polygamy**. The empire was scoured for officials who had knowledge of the West, particularly those who spoke English or French. These he employed in high positions in court and government.

Modernizing or Westernizing?

If, by the middle of the 19th century, European leaders thought that the Ottoman Empire was about to embrace Western values, they were mistaken. Mahmud was happy to borrow what he needed from the West, but only in order to make his empire into a modern world power.

After Mahmud's death in 1839, modernization continued, although it was becoming clear that even with reforms, the Ottoman Empire, as it was, could not survive long into the 20th century. Abdul Aziz, Mahmud's second son, was the first sultan to visit Europe. In 1867, he visited Paris, then London, but the trade agreements he made there just added to the empire's problems. The empire was in debt and about to go to war again. When Empress Eugénie of France returned Aziz's visit, there was a sudden demand for European fashions and fabrics created by the rush to emulate the empress' Parisian dresses. Wealthy ladies now wanted imported silk for their dresses, rather than silk made locally. There was an increased demand for European goods generally, and it seemed inevitable that the empire would continue to soak up influences from the West until nothing of its own culture remained.

In many rural areas of modern Turkey, costumes similar to these are still worn. The soft leather shoes with the turned-up toes are called *yemeni*.

It was Mustafa Kemal—also known as Kemal Atatürk—who saved what was left of the old Ottoman Empire and reshaped it into a new Turkish republic. Kemal banned all Islamic-style costumes, saying: "This grotesque mixture of styles is neither national nor international. A civilized dress is worthy of our nation, and we will wear it." Kemal believed that a more modern costume would help Turkey to look forward to the future rather than to the past. He was not accepting the Westernization of his nation: he was doing the same as Greeks, Byzantines, and Ottomans had all done previously, which was to take and adapt what they liked from other cultures and make it their own.

Glossary

Note: Specialized words relating to clothing are explained within the text, but those that appear more than once are listed below for easy reference.

Acropolis the upper fortified part of an ancient Greek city

Aesthetic having a highly developed appreciation of beauty

Austere basic or disciplined

Bolt roll of cloth

Breeches short pants covering the hips and thighs and fitting snugly at the lower edges at or just below the knee

Brocade fabric with a raised pattern

Brooch an ornament held by a pin or clasp and worn at or near the neck

Caftan long, coat-like robe worn in Persia

Cassock a close-fitting ankle-length garment worn by the clergy and by laymen

Chemise long, tight Byzantine undergarment with sleeves

Chiton a Greek garment made from a long rectangle of finely woven wool; it was folded over the body and pinned at the shoulders to make a short knee-length tunic

Corselet a piece of armor covering the lower part of the torso

Cuirass a piece of armor covering the body from neck to waist

Democracy a government by the people

Diadem crown-like band, usually decorated with a single hanging jewel

Dominance the fact of having control over something

Edict law

Ferace a long, flowing, ankle-length robe worn by Turkish women

Fez a brimless red hat worn by Turkish men, but later also adopted by women

Flax a plant whose fiber is used for spinning

Girdle sash worn by Greeks and Romans

Greaves armor worn on the shins

Imam leader of prayer in a mosque

Janissaries slave soldiers in the Ottoman army

Kethüda official position held by a female as a general overseer of staff performance in various departments

Minaret slim tower of a mosque

Monopoly complete control

Mosque a building used for public worship by Muslims

Motif repeating theme or idea

Nomad a person who has no fixed residence, but moves from place to place, usually seasonally and within a well-defined territory

Pallium a simple draped tunic, similar to those worn by Greek philosophers

Patriarchs major bishops in the Greek Orthodox Church

Pelpos a female version of the simple Doric *chiton*

Piety devotion to God

Polygamy the practice of having more than one spouse at a time

Regalia robes or emblems of high office

Relic holy object, such as a saint's bone or a fragment of Christ's cross

Salvars baggy pants that narrowed at the ankles, commonly worn by Turkish men

Spindle a round stick with tapered ends used to form and twist the yarn in the hand

Standard an object carried at the top of a pole and used to mark a rallying point or serve as an emblem

Strait a narrow passageway connecting two large bodies of water

Textile a woven or knitted cloth

Vestments priestly clothing used for ceremonies

Vizier a high executive officer in the Ottoman Empire

Whelk a large marine snail

Timeline

1200 B.C.	The Dorians arrive in southern Greece, driving the Ionians out of their traditional homelands and into Attica.
1100	Growth of Greek city-states begins.
800	Start of Greek civilization.
753	Rome is founded.
477–431	"Golden Age" of Greek civilization.
146	The Roman armies of Emperor Antonius Pius conquer the region.
A.D. 324	Constantine establishes "New Rome" in Byzantium.
330	Byzantium is rechristened Constantinople.
395	Western Roman Empire splits from East; Byzantine empire is born.
476	End of Roman Empire.
1204	"Rape of Constantinople."
1326	Osman's Turks found the Ottoman Empire.
1453	Mehmed II captures Constantinople; end of Byzantine empire.
1821–1829	Greek war of independence.
1832	Otto I becomes first Greek king.
1867	Abdul Aziz is the first sultan to visit Europe.
1908	"Young Turks" force Sultan to create new Ottoman constitution.
1918	Ottoman Empire is occupied by Allies after its defeat in World War I.
1922	Ottoman Empire is dissolved.
1923	Turkish republic is founded.

Online Sources

Ancient Greece
www.historylink101.com/ancient_greece.html
A good, well-designed site containing links on all topics, including ancient Greek art and architecture, famous people, mythology, and everyday life.

Ancient Greece and Its Environs Costumes Links
www.costumes.org/pages/greekslinks.html
An excellent site that gives students a good starting point for further independent research.

Greek Costume through the Centuries
http://milieux.com/costume/
Images and text that take the reader through 4,000 years of Greek costume, from the ancient Minoans to the clothing of Queen Amalia in the mid-19th century.

Internet Sourcebooks
This ever-growing online resource has extensive links and is ideal for students.

For information on:
Byzantium and the Ottoman Empire, see
www.fordham.edu/halsall/sbooklc.html
(The Medieval Sourcebook).

The Ottoman Empire, Greece, and Turkey during the 18th and 19th centuries, see
www.fordham.edu/halsall/mod/modsbook.html
(The Modern History Sourcebook).

Ottoman Islamic culture, see
www.fordham.edu/halsall/islam/islambook/html
(The Islamic Sourcebook).

Further Reading

Barrow, Reginald Hayes, *The Romans.* Middlesex: Penguin, 1985.

Barton, Lucy. *Historic Costume for the Stage.* London: A & C Black, 1963.

Coco, Carla. *Secrets of the Harem.* New York: Vendome Press, 1999.

Dubois, Jill. *Greece (Cultures of the World).* New York: Marshall Cavendish Corporation, 2003.

Goodwin, Godfrey. *The Private World of Ottoman Women.* London: S.A.Q.I., 1997.

Hornblower, Simon and Antony Spawforth. *The Oxford Companion to Classical Civilisation.* Oxford: Oxford University Press, 1998.

Inalcik, Halil. *The Ottoman Empire: The Classical Age 1300–1600.* London: Phoenix, 1994.
Kitto, Humphrey David Findlay. *The Greeks.* New York: Penguin, 1951.

Nicolle, David and Angus McBride. *Men at Arms: Armies of the Ottoman Empire 1775–1820.* Oxford: Osprey Military, 2000.

Paul, Penelope. *Legacies: Costume and Clothes.* East Sussex: Wayland, 1995.

Vance, Peggy. *Illustrated History of European Costume: Period Styles and Accessories.* London: Collins & Brown, 2000.

Yarwood, Doreen. *European Costume: 4000 Years of Fashion.* London: Batsford, 1975.

About the Author

Paula Hammond was born and educated in the ancient Roman town of Chester, England. After completing a degree in History, Literature, and Theology at Trinity College, she moved to London to pursue a career in publishing. Her writing credits include *Communication Through The Ages*, which traces the history of writing and communication, and *The Grubbiest Adventure...Ever*, a project-based research resource for young children. She is currently writing a series for teenagers on notable historical figures and events.

Index